CRYSTAL TAGGART, MBA

THE FUTURE OF PROFIT

Copyright © 2017 by Crystal Taggart.

All rights reserved. No part of this publication may be reproduced, distributed or transmitted in any form or by any means, including photocopying, recording, or other electronic or mechanical methods, without the prior written permission of the publisher, except in the case of brief quotations embodied in critical reviews and certain other noncommercial uses permitted by copyright law. For permission requests, write to the publisher, addressed "Attention: Permissions Coordinator," at the address below.

Crystal Taggart
64 E. Broadway Ste 206
Phoenix, AZ 85282
www.atlasinnovations.com

Book Layout ©2017 BookDesignTemplates.com

The AI Revolution: The Future of Profit by Crystal Taggart. —1st ed.
ISBN 978-1975653323

Contents

Introduction 5
    Machine Learning 9
    Computer Vision 11
    Natural Language Processing 14
    Virtual Agents 15
    Deep Learning 16
    Smart Robotics 20
    Robotic Process Automation (RPA) 21
    Preparing for the Revolution 22
    Looking for Opportunities 24

AI Technologies 26
    Coding Languages 26
    Frameworks 28
    Platforms 29
    Types of Learning 31

RPA Technologies 33
    RPA Market Leaders 34

Planning an RPA Project 36

RPA Solution Maturity 40

Potential Problems 42

Payback Timeframe 43

The Future of RPA 44

Machine Learning 46

    Creating a Model 46

    Model Identification 48

    Model Training 48

    Deployment 49

    Examples 50

    Bias in Machine Learning 51

Deep Learning 53

    Examples 54

    Problems 55

Chatbots/Virtual Agents 57

    Superbots 58

    Shopping Bots 59

Business Bots 60

App-based bots 60

Using Bots for Your Business 61

Chatbot Development Platforms 63

Implementing Bots in Your Organization 65

Computer Vision 71

Computer Vision Technologies 72

Examples 75

Natural Language Processing 76

NLP Solutions 77

Challenges with NLP 80

Examples 81

I've Been Vetted Case Study 84

JP Morgan Case Study 86

Eddie the Sales Robot 88

Next Steps 90

Hold on to your butts.

—Ray Arnold, Jurassic Park

CHAPTER 1

Introduction

The phrases 'Machine Learning' and 'Artificial Intelligence' have been hyped for years with the expectation that The Jetsons will suddenly become a reality with talking robots that will clean our house and passive-aggressively perform our jobs. That reality is closer than you think and will evolve in ways that you won't expect. For some people, this creates new opportunities. For many people, this will create huge amounts of turmoil and be the cause for new programs like Universal Basic Income to be implemented.

The robots are coming.

In the near future, jobs that used to exist will be replaced by robots and AI. New job assignments will be focused on exception management, creative tasks, and tasks that are not cost effective for automation.

Why should you care? By 2023 it's expected that AI will be as smart as a person and by 2045 it's expected that AI will be smarter than all brains combined on earth. What this means is that dramatic change is coming quickly and companies that aren't participating will be quickly left behind.

The unfortunate fact of AI is that it was created by mathematicians and statisticians (who are awesome) but have a hard time explaining what they are talking about to the rest of us. The goal of this book is to demystify the geek-speak and highly technical jargon and explain what exciting advances that are taking place in AI today that can be capitalized on now.

Today's landscape of AI is complex and hard to apply to practical business problems. Most examples of AI highlighted in the news are impractical use cases for most businesses. I guess it's interesting that a Google robot taught itself to walk in a video game, but that's not particularly helpful for me and my business. You also see tech superstars like Elon Musk talking to the media every week about the impending AI 'doomsday' while simultaneously launching companies that want to integrate the human brain with a computer[1].

I, for one, am excited about these changes. When it's 99% safe to install my super computer chip into my brain, sign me up! My husband may *hate* that since I would be right 100% of the time instead of 99.9% of the time but, this highlights just one way that AI is going to transform our society in dramatic ways very rapidly.

We are in an unprecedented time of change, and this is the very beginning. The major tech companies have launched solutions that make it easier than ever to create AI solutions. The cloud computing power has dramatically reduced the cost of implementation, with many of the leading AI platforms being open sourced. With these changes will also come dramatic social change as well.

There are estimates that unemployment will range from 20-50% within the next ten years. Entire industries will be transformed causing massive unemployment. The White House estimates that 2-3 million jobs will be displaced, solely from the self-driving car industry. For people in those jobs today who aren't replaced, they will likely move into lesser roles with less pay.

The White House states "Advances in Artificial Intelligence (AI) technology and related fields have opened up new markets and new opportunities for progress in critical areas such as health, education, energy, economic inclusion, social welfare, and the environment. In recent years, machines have surpassed humans in the performance of certain tasks related to intelligence, such as aspects of image recognition. Experts forecast that rapid progress in the field of specialized artificial intelligence will continue. Although it is unlikely that machines will exhibit broadly-applicable intelligence comparable to or exceeding that of humans in the next 20 years, it is to be expected that machines will continue to reach and exceed human performance on more and more tasks."[2]

The major areas of change that research firm McKinsey[3] identifies as key VC investment areas in AI-focused companies are:

- Machine Learning (5-7B)
- Computer Vision (2.5-3.5B)
- Natural Language (.6-.9B)
- Autonomous Vehicles (.3-.5B)
- Smart Robotics (.3-.5B)
- Virtual Agents (.1-.2B)

In most organizations, AI will likely end up being a painful and clumsy evolution, *not a revolution*. However, companies that fail to take on the learning curve that AI presents will be disrupted with new innovative products.

With the influx of tech giants making AI accessible to companies of any size, AI will soon become table stakes for companies wanting to compete in the modern digital economy. Four major players in the market provide over 75% of the cloud computing capabilities and they all offer Machine Learning and AI products. With companies such as Amazon (41%) Microsoft (29%) Google (3%) and IBM (2.9%) creating offerings in this space, the entry point to set up and deploy scalable, production-ready solutions instantly is significantly less.

AI is truly an evolution that will take time to adopt and implement. I'll start off with a summary of each of the core AI technologies and what they do.

Machine Learning

Machine learning is the practice of using an algorithm to predict an outcome. At its core, machine learning is a set of math formulas that identify statistical probabilities and give you deep insights into massive amounts of data. Steeped in calculus and statistics formulas, machine learning provides the capability to understand your information and create probabilities that relate information, predict outcomes, segment customers, and recommend products. Machine learning can also be referred to as predictive analytics.

Machine learning differs from traditional programming in many ways. Traditional programs define a predetermined set of business rules to determine outcomes and make decisions. Machine learning focuses on probabilities to make decisions, and those decisions improve over time based on the quantity and quality of data you have.

Industries such as finance and banking have been using machine learning for years. Fraud detection and credit score models contain complex algorithms that have analyzed billions of records to determine if it's you that purchased something or if you will repay your car loan.

Retailers have been using machine learning algorithms for markdown optimization (used typically when prices reduce on seasonal items). Previously, these platforms were only available as add-ons to expensive ERP platforms. With today's machine learning capabilities and historical data, even small retailers can implement pricing optimization without a multi-million-dollar software implementation.

Most companies are not using the data they have today. The current metric from Cisco is that 99.5% of data is never analyzed and companies are sitting on a wealth of information that they can learn about their customers.[4] Machine learning makes this analysis much easier.

The next generation of machine learning solutions will enable the smallest merchants to create offers instantly based on customer history, demographics and psychographics.

IOT (Internet of Things) systems will be able to use inexpensive sensors to track anything that can be tracked and machine learning algorithms will be able to instantly determine anomalies based on historical information. Examples of this include heavy equipment maintenance solutions that detect employee abuse of equipment or solutions that detect maintenance issues and create repair requests automatically.

The range of machine learning solutions can vary greatly, but can support everything from customer churn prediction to pricing analytics to marketing spend analytics to project ROI assessment analytics. Within every department in an organization, machine learning has the capability to improve decision-making across the board.

Computer Vision

Computer vision is the ability to take photographic or video information and analyze the data instantly for various insights. Computer vision also uses machine learning algorithms to determine probabilities that one thing matches another. Older solutions focused on handwriting analytics or OCR technologies which take text from forms and populate databases. Newer solutions are used in health tech software such as a skin-cancer detecting algorithm that is currently being developed by the IBM Watson team[5]. This solution takes a photo of a lesion and compares the image with other dermoscopy images to identify the correlation of melanoma in the photo. The technology today does 'as well at recognizing disease in the dataset as specialists.'[5]

Numerous cancer research computer vision solutions are currently under development, making it easier, less expensive, and less error prone to detect cancer early. With these types of technologies, a cancer-detecting app is just around the corner.

The next generation of computer vision technologies will not only dramatically affect the healthcare industry, but will also be ever-present in our daily lives. Billboards will be able to detect the types of cars driving by on the freeway and statistically calculate the demographics for ads that will reach prime demographics during peak driving times.

Even today you can download the Bare Minerals app, take a photo of your skin to get a custom makeup composition for your unique skin tone. What's even more fascinating (and slightly horrifying) is that with the information that Bare Minerals collects, they'll be able to identify detailed information about their users including pore size, age, ethnicity, and body hair. Using geolocation services, they'll also be able to collect insights into socio-economic status, all with little-to-no effort other than just storing the data in a table.

A useful OCR solution called CamCard allows you to scan a business card at an event and instantly creates a contact in your email account for your new contact. They use OCR technologies to create the contact but their algorithms aren't perfect. The genius of CamCard is that you are prompted to correct the data which gives them two things:

1. An accurate database of contacts and companies that they can sell to the highest bidder.
2. The ability to re-train their algorithms to fix inaccuracies and improve their computer vision IP.

Ebay recently added a 'search by image' feature that allows their users to take a photo from their phone and search through their billions of listings to find what you are looking for.

Facebook has been using computer vision technologies for years including automatically tagging friends and using friends tagged photos as security questions for password resets.

Computer vision is a crucial capability in self-driving cars, enabling the cars to process 360-degrees of information and make decisions such as stopping, going, slowing, and changing lanes.

Computer vision is even being used in farming technologies with robots being used to plant seeds, water plants and pull weeds.

Startup Smart Eye provides non-invasive eye tracking solutions that enable a broad range of applications. Smart Eye is testing solutions for integration to cars for driver identification and safety applications such as drowsy driver alerts. Today marketers use heat maps on pages to determine where people focus their attention on a web page. The heat maps of tomorrow will be expanded using eye tracking technologies that will measure responses to advertising and product packaging to test multiple campaigns.

Imagine walking down a city street where a digital sign captures your image, what you are wearing, determines your demographics and psychographics, then adjusts its signage accordingly. Then as you look at the sign, it tracks your eye movements and then as you walk by subsequent signs it 'recognizes you' and then repeats the signage and adjusts the copy based on where you looked last, or adjusts the signage altogether.

This may sound like science fiction but the technologies to make this happen are here today and are not that difficult to implement. It just hasn't been commercialized and scaled yet.

Natural Language Processing

Natural language processing is the ability to take unstructured documents and comments that have been lying around collecting dust for years and create real insights into that information. Natural language solutions typically target creating categories or related information based on categorized datasets. For example, creating keywords for searches based on article content or finding related documents based on language contained in the text.

Spam filters have been using natural language processing for years to detect spam and move email to the spam box. Newer AI companies such as X.ai have developed Amy (who could also be considered a Virtual Agent), an AI bot that schedules meetings on your behalf. Simply cc amy@x.ai in your email request and she will perform the back and forth to find a time on your calendar to meet.

Many organizations have portals, shared drives, PDFs and word documents all with terabytes of unstructured text data waiting for companies to access it.

The natural language processing solutions of the future will integrate to your email system and automatically generate things like email responses, assign tasks and reminders to teammates, create employee reviews based on both project results and cultural indicators of success (i.e. how the employee responds to their internal or external customers, do they respond with a good attitude and positive sentiments?)

The HRIS solutions of the future will read and interpret resumes, automatically interview employees, monitor the emails of those candidates hired and then automatically determine who is on a path for promotion and who is on a path for termination.

Virtual Agents

When most people think of AI, this is what people expect that AI is – a robot that interacts with you. Ranging from a friendly robot that serves you dinner to a WestWorld experience where a robotic person interacts with you and creates experiences.

The old version of virtual agents were phone systems that ask questions and interpret the answer (such as your bank phone system asking 'Why are you calling today?') The current evolution of virtual agents will be focused in the chat bot and customer service arenas.

Companies like Kik are finding traction with marketing to young audiences and recommending products for purchase. Kik is a messaging platform that lets teens chat with each other. Their platform allows companies to integrate chatbot functionality into the messaging experience to enable teens to see H&M's look of the day or other types of messaging integrations. Companies such as Slack and Facebook have created a bot-friendly ecosystem where you can introduce bots that order you an Uber or tell you the weather.

The next generation of virtual agents will combine technologies such as natural language processing and personalized scripting to create user experiences that seamlessly interact with people to provide service and answer questions. These agents will be initially clumsy, but as the tools evolve, will be able to learn from their human counterparts and correctly answer similar questions in the future.

Since marketers are always looking for new innovative ways to reach their customers, the chatbot arms race will soon begin with major retailers all competing for ways to get you to talk to their chatbot who, in turn, will be happy to sell you something.

Deep Learning

Deep Learning is set of algorithms that learns from the data over time and modifies your algorithms to create weighted data over time. These algorithms recognize patterns in the data, then subsequent levels identify patterns in the patterns.

Deep Learning models are modeled after the human brain. Our neurons take small pieces of information then connect it with information known by other neurons in the network and then make a prediction. Deep Learning uses neural networks which take one or more inputs (information), weights them over time (knowledge) to create an output (prediction.)

A common use case for deep learning is for predicting customer churn. A machine learning model can predict customer churn as well, but the models work differently.

In a machine learning model, you would plug in your data and determine what data is correlated to your churn rate (age, gender, salary, zip code and other demographics, order totals, etc.)

A machine learning model would create a model with a math formula that looks like this:

> Customers between the ages of 18-24 have a 30% chance of churn
>
> Customers between the ages of 24-35 have a 20% chance of churn
>
> Customers older than 35 have a 90% chance of churn.

A company with this information can create marketing campaigns that send proactive offers to engage customers that meet the churn criteria and can create advertising campaigns that target customers between 24-35 since they are likely to stay with the product.

In the same example, a Deep Learning model would take each customer record and determine the churn. They would create models from data like this:

Age	Gender	Duration	Churned
19	F	2 years	N
21	F	3 years	N
20	M	1 week	Y
25	M	1 week	Y
27	F	10 years	N
29	F	9 years	N
31	M	1 week	Y

The model would take each variable (gender, age, length of relationship) and predict if they stayed or churned and would weight the variables based on importance. From this analysis, you can create new business processes to 'save the sale' and have this targeted to specific demographics. You can also make better predictions on which customers you should target in paid media campaigns.

In this scenario, a deep learning algorithm could determine that the age when someone becomes a customer is 17-20 and is usually female. It would assign a higher probability of retaining a customer for someone meeting those qualities than a male in the same age range.

Deep Learning is used by Google in several of their algorithms from everything from search algorithms to predicting search phrases to image recognition. Deep learning can be used in everything from business prediction and classification to computer vision image processing solutions to recommender systems, like systems used by Netflix.

The use case for Netflix is different than most. For Amazon's recommender algorithms, they can recommend a product that you might be interested in and they don't lose anything if you choose an alternate product. If it comes from Amazon, they make margin. In Netflix's case, because their movie catalogue is predicated on obscure non-blockbuster hits, they had to optimize their models for movies that aren't the blockbusters, but indie films related to other people who liked movies similar to your tastes. Netflix states that their recommender algorithm has earned them over a billion dollars in customer retention.

Autonomous Vehicles

Autonomous vehicles are already here, they just aren't legally accepted yet by the states (but are currently being tested in farming operations.) Google's self-driving car started in 2005 with a $2m grant and in 2014 was revealed to be fully automated. When they unveiled their new car with no steering wheel, gas pedal or brake pedal (to the horror of lawmakers everywhere) they set a new precedent in the driverless car movement.

Now rebranded as Waymo, these cars are being actively tested. Today, autonomous vehicles have already achieved a safer level of driving than humans with over a million miles logged with a total 14 accidents, all but 2 of which were caused by a human driver and the other two of which were caused by obstructions in the road. Uber has launched a similar test with driverless cars.

Between the automation of these vehicles and automated drones delivering packages to your home (Amazon is actively working on their drone delivery project), these are the areas that will have the greatest economic impact near-term. These technologies will disrupt millions of jobs, while also making us safer on the road.

Smart Robotics

Robotics were responsible for the first major industry disruption with jobs declining in manufacturing by 35% since they were introduced in the 80's[6].

Robotics have been proven to dramatically increase productivity and accuracy as well. Recently a factory in China replaced 90% of their human workforce with robotics and reported a 250% increase in productivity and an 80% drop in defects[7].

With more access to technology with movements like the Maker movement which give entrepreneurs access to low-cost chips for research and development, new innovations will be easier to realize where even hobbyists will be able to design their own robots.

Crowdfunding sites such as Kickstarter have become the launchpad for new companies, making it easier than ever for a company to validate their product without a major investment.

Technologies such as 3D printing that are now accessible to anyone with a few hundred dollars are going to create new industries of instant customization. Combined with technologies such as computer vision, a repair technician will be able to print a replacement part and install it - all without leaving the site. These technologies are expanding into other materials and uses such as food preparation (Holiday Inn makes printed pancakes for their patrons), housing, and even makeup (Judy Jetson's instant fingernail painters are already available.)

Robotic Process Automation (RPA)

Robotic process automation isn't really an AI technology, but using RPA *combined with* AI solutions can create very powerful tools for business automation. An RPA process is a scripted process that is used to interact with existing computer applications for business process automation. A typical example is automation for data entry tasks such as claims processing but extend to every business department. RPA can be used for onboarding new employees, IT support requests, accounts payable tasks, and sales and marketing automation.

By integrating RPA processes with machine learning algorithms, RPA can become a 'smart robot' and make decisions using machine learning and deep learning algorithms, instead of using hard-coded business rules. These machines can gain the ability to become more accurate than many clerical workers and would make better data-based decisions than a person could.

Another advantage to these solutions is that they monitor their own results, so you get real numbers on productivity and their error rates. The robots aren't afraid to share their shortcomings and they provide their own performance reviews. They are also designed to work with legacy applications including windows applications, web applications, SAP applications, and in virtual environments which means you can use your existing applications and existing business processes for automation and then immediately make your employees more productive.

Preparing for the Revolution

In preparation for these upcoming shifts in technology, Udacity is now offering 'nanodegrees' in each of these technologies so companies can find and hire employees to support these new capabilities. Companies such as Google, IBM, Mercedes Benz, and Bosch have teamed up with Udacity to create targeted training with the hope that a ready workforce will mean more adoption of their technologies.

When implementing these technologies, it's not a revolution but an *evolution*. Companies who are looking for natural language processing expertise start with machine learning fundamentals to understand their data better. Companies creating advanced autonomous vehicles started with a computer vision foundation.

There will be opportunities to leapfrog the learning curve by implementing AI algorithms as part of packaged software implementations - companies such as Saleforce.com, Zendesk, and Hubspot are already implementing AI within their technology stacks. By waiting for these other companies to lead the way, there are several risks to your business:

- If you aren't experimenting with AI technologies today, you won't understand how they work or what they are doing when they are added to your packaged applications.
- Your competitors are likely experimenting with these technologies and improving their results based on insights provided by AI technologies.
- Your competitors are overcoming the learning curve sooner. Today, AI is new and novel and forgivable when it's not perfect. Companies adopting AI are in a

better position to evolve to create seamless experiences for their customers.
- If you are waiting for packaged software enhancements, then you'll have the same capabilities as your competitors at the same time they do. There's no competitive advantage to waiting.
- Companies that use AI technologies are trusted more by younger generations.
- These new technologies will quickly become 'table stakes' in many industries - if you haven't adopted it you can't compete.

Looking for Opportunities

Every business should be looking for opportunities to expand (or begin!) their knowledge on AI capabilities. Recently, a McKinsey article stated that 41% of companies are uncertain of the benefits of AI. However, companies that adopted AI as a key technology strategy perform 3-15% better on average measured by profit margins.

For companies looking for opportunities, McKinsey recommends focusing on some key areas:

- R&D
- Forecasting
- Optimizing production and maintenance
- Targeted sales and marketing efforts
- Improving user experiences across all channels

McKinsey states that companies who are successfully adopting AI have some key attributes including identifying useful use cases, an extensive data ecosystem, access to tools, workflow processes that can be integrated into AI technologies, and open cultures that adapt to change.

Companies that have high AI adoption include High Tech/Telecom firms, Automotive, and Financial services. Medium AI adoption includes Retail, Media, and CPG firms. While education, healthcare and travel industries have low AI adoption.

Companies who invest in AI can gain a new distinct competitive advantage over their low-tech counterparts. Healthcare companies are seeing the largest gains in these areas with most AI leaders expecting current returns to increase by up to 5% more than industry average[3].

Long story short, if you aren't looking for opportunities to explore AI and aren't investing in your AI capabilities, be prepared to be left behind.

Notes

[1] https://neuralink.com/

[2] https://www.whitehouse.gov/sites/whitehouse.gov/files/images/EMBARGOED%20AI%20Economy%20Report.pdf

[3] http://www.mckinsey.com/~/media/McKinsey/Industries/Advanced%20Electronics/Our%20Insights/How%20artificial%20intelligence%20can%20deliver%20real%20value%20to%20companies/MGI-Artificial-Intelligence-Discussion-paper.ashx

[4] https://www.cisco.com/c/dam/r/en/us/internet-of-everything-ioe/analytics-automation/assets/files/analytics-infographic.pdf

[5] https://www.ibm.com/blogs/research/2016/11/identifying-skin-cancer-computer-vision/

[6] https://fred.stlouisfed.org/series/MANEMP

[7] http://www.businessinsider.com/companys-productivity-soared-after-replacing-90-of-employees-with-robots-2017-2

CHAPTER 2

AI Technologies

The technologies used in machine learning are comprised of a number of components including programming languages, the frameworks used (which provide out-of-the box algorithms ready to implement), and platforms used for hosting services.

This is the most technical section of this book, but necessary to set the foundation for the business implications relative to implementing machine learning and AI models.

When a data scientist tells you that they need the Cuda framework installed on an AWS GPU machine with Theano and Tensorflow (and that it costs $650/month to develop on a GPU machine), then you'll understand what that means.

Coding Languages

Python

Python is the most common coding language that supports machine learning. Most platforms support Python. Python not only supports AI capability, but is also used for full-scale application development on websites and API services.

Python is a better solution when you are ready to productionalize your code and deploy machine learning services since most organizations already have an infrastructure that supports Python deployments. Since Python is open-source, it's also a low-cost way to deploy new servers to support new business capabilities.

R

R is another coding language used to create machine learning models. Whereas most production models use Python as their core language for production deployment, R is typically used by statisticians to clean and analyze data. R is a platform created specifically for statistical analysis for academics. R also comes with several reporting visualization libraries that are used to display the results of your data analysis with beautiful charts and graphs.

Most applications use Python or R for most business applications. Most data scientists prefer Python over R due to the fact that Python is a true programming language that allows you to extend your data model into services for use in your applications. Most statisticians like R because of its rich reporting capabilities. Many data scientists will use R to clean and transform their data, then move to Python when they are ready to deploy their models to production.

Companies such as Microsoft support both Python and R in their machine learning platforms.

C/C++

Certain libraries targeted toward heavy graphics and image processing use C++ as the language of choice. Companies with highly specialized AI applications in medical image processing, search engines, and self-driving cars focus on C++.

Frameworks

There are many libraries that are used with Python and R that provide algorithms for data processing. Typically, a data scientist will use multiple frameworks to solve a specific problem - a technique called ensemble learning. Coding languages such as Python use frameworks for their core algorithms.

Theano

Theano is an open source framework developed by the University of Montreal. Theano is primarily used for numerical computation and calculations on massive data sets. The advantage to using Theano over traditional Python libraries is that it runs on both a computer with a CPU, and can be run on GPUs, which has exponentially more computing capabilities and is specialized for parallel computations. Theano is considered the most wide-spread library.

Tensorflow

Tensorflow is an open source framework developed by Google. Tensorflow also runs on CPU or GPUs. Tensorflow also is used for fast numerical computations and calculations on massive datasets. Since Tensorflow is backed by Google, it's quickly gaining adoption and traction.

Keras

Keras is an open source framework that use Theano and Tensorflow libraries to quickly build deep learning models with a few lines of code. Keras was developed by François Chollet who is a machine learning science at Google.

Caffe

Caffe is an open source framework developed by the Berkeley Vision and Learning Center and was designed to be a fast model for deep learning and image processing. Caffe is designed to easily upgrade from CPU processing for development to GPU processing for full-scale deployments.

Torch

Torch is designed to create machine-learning applications that are deployed to local machines. They offer a set of frameworks for Mac, Windows, Linux and Android which enables developers to deploy applications that use machine learning algorithms without communicating back to a server for computations. This is heavily used in applications that process audio and video data. Torch uses a programming language called Lua and can also use C.

Platforms

There are many platforms that provide and specialize in hosting machine learning and AI applications. We are just covering 'the big 5' since they are the most adopted platforms in this space.

IBM Watson

IBM Watson has created several different platforms targeting multiple segments including Health, Commerce, Financial Services, IOT, Supply Chain, Marketing and HR. IBM provides an analytics platform and machine learning platform through their Bluemix service that enables companies to deploy machine learning services. They also offer many APIs focused on computer vision, speech to text, sentiment analysis, and translation that are supported in many programming languages.

Google Cloud

The Google Cloud platform has segmented their pricing based on what your model is doing, either training or predicting. Google charges based on the time your model takes to train and then charges based on the number of API calls that use the model. Google is designed for Tensorflow algorithms. Google also provides GPU servers where Tensorflow and other AI frameworks can be deployed for production.

Amazon Machine Learning

On Amazon, you can deploy machine learning by implementing a framework on an AWS server (for example installing Python and Tensorflow on an AWS server), or you can use Amazon's machine learning services which provides tools for data analysis and visualization, data cleansing, model performance visualizations, and data transformations.

Microsoft Machine Learning and Cognitive Services

Microsoft's Machine Learning is comprised of a hosted Azure machine learning server. In addition to this, much like IBM, Microsoft is providing API services that offer capabilities with computer vision, speech to text, sentiment, and recommendations. Microsoft's API services are largely in preview mode at the time of this writing.

Adobe Spark

Adobe Spark is an open source platform that is optimized for the mathematical calculations required for machine learning algorithms. Apache Spark is supported by IBM who has contributed 3500 developers[1] to contribute to the Apache Spark source code. Developers code in either PySpark (Python with Spark libraries) or Scala.

Types of Learning

There are three ways where machine learning algorithms are created called supervised learning, unsupervised learning and reinforcement learning. We'll describe what each of those means at a high level.

Supervised

Supervised models start with a data scientist who reviews the data, cleans up junk or missing data (this is typically one of the largest portions of a machine learning project) and then creates a model. They evaluate the results of the model, often running it through different types of algorithms to determine which model best predicts the results. This is the most common process of creating machine learning applications today.

Unsupervised

Unsupervised models start with an unlabeled dataset and the machine learning and deep learning algorithms learn to create predictions. Unsupervised learning algorithms are used commonly for clustering, when you want to group your data based on the information provided. An example of this would be a customer segmentation list.

Reinforcement Learning

Reinforcement learning provides the highest level of AI programming and is commonly used to build models from scratch. Reinforcement learning takes in information and learns from interactions with its environment.

The Google team created a reinforcement learning platform that beat the world champion of the game Go in 2016[2]. The primary difference between Google's champion Go player and IBM Watson's champion chess player in 1997 was that Watson was pre-programmed with a catalog of strategies which were then used to statistically calculate probabilities of success for winning.

Google's Go algorithm learned how to win the game by *playing itself*. This is considered one of the most historic moments for artificial intelligence. Google's AI company DeepMind created an AI platform that taught itself to walk using positive and negative reinforcement.

Reinforcement learning is commonly used in recommendation systems. The advantage that a reinforcement system offers over other methods is that other types of learning are targeted towards averages meaning that 'most people who choose X also choose Y. Reinforcement algorithms can be used to create personalization services targeted toward individuals[3].

To wrap this all up in a nice little bow, a data scientist uses Python with Keras (which uses a Tensorflow framework) to create a supervised learning model hosted on Google cloud using GPU processing for faster performance.

Notes

[1] https://techcrunch.com/2015/06/15/ibm-pours-researchers-and-resources-into-apache-spark-project/

[2] https://techcrunch.com/2016/03/17/google-defeating-go-champion-shows-ai-can-find-solutions-humans-dont-see/

[3] https://mondaynote.com/deepmind-could-bring-the-best-news-recommendation-engine-fc66051cf2ca

CHAPTER 3

RPA Technologies

RPA Technologies are often confused with Business Process Management (BPM) solutions (and often are offered as a solution within a BPM suite.) The key differentiator between RPA and BPM solutions are two major areas:

- BPMS solutions typically require business process re-engineering and complex integrations to be coded to support the solution.
- RPA solutions are designed to automate existing business processes using existing applications for faster delivery and execution.

The website WillRobotsTakeMyJob.com[1] identifies different jobs that will be automated. Some highlights include:

- First-Line Supervisors of Housekeepers and Janitors: "You are doomed or 94% probability of automation"
- Stationary Engineers and Boiler Operators: "Robots are watching or 89% probability of automation"
- Middle School Teachers: "Start worrying or 26% probability of automation"

Automation is coming and it's coming quickly. A study conducted by Oxford in 2013 identified that 47% of jobs will be replaced by robots within the next twenty years[2] with the highest risk areas identified as transportation, production, and office and administrative support.

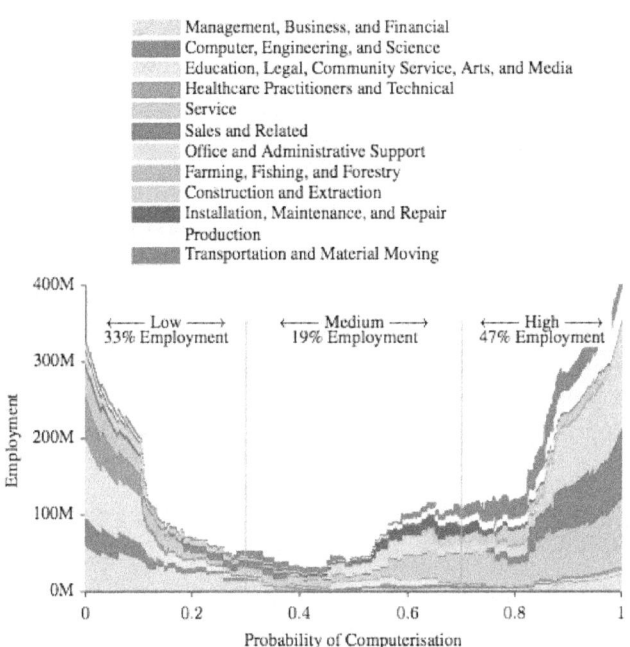

Source: Oxford, The Future of Employment[2]

RPA Market Leaders

In the most recent Forrester Wave report[3] on RPA, there are three major market leaders in the RPA space.

At the time of this writing, only UI Path offers the capability to download a free trial version of the product to experiment with RPA technologies. Both UI Path and Automation Anywhere offer free training for their platforms.

UIPath

UIPath has an easy and intuitive interface for RPA creation and training documentation that is geared towards non-technical users. With minor understanding of programming and scripting, it's easy to quickly automate business processes across several applications and platforms.

UIPath supports remote bot management and execution, meaning that a centralized robot platform schedules and monitors robot results. Coenraad Van at UI Path states that their platform is both robust in how it handles unstructured data and is extensible, meaning that it can handle a large variety of automations and can easily integrate to existing platforms and AI frameworks to add value to the robots created.

Automation Anywhere

Automation Anywhere is an RPA platform that targets processes such as cash to quote, procure to pay in heavy ERP packages. Automation Anywhere has over 10,000 certified developers. Automation Anywhere requires some level of programming expertise to be successful in their platform. With Automation Anywhere's IQBot, they have included machine learning capabilities integrated directly in their platform.

Blue Prism

Blue Prism is one of the first companies who identified a distinction between BPM (Business Process Management) capabilities and RPA capabilities and their go to market strategy focused in the RPA space. They have central management and queue management capabilities that enable companies to assign work to a bot, the same as they would a person.

Planning an RPA Project

When planning your first RPA project, it should align with a broader organizational strategy regarding your AI and automation roadmaps.

There are three major phases for implementing RPA in an organization:

- Experimentation and Identification
- Enterprise Roadmap Definition
- Center of Excellence

Experimentation/Identification

Van states that there's an evolution of how RPA is implemented. The first phase of implementation begins with experimentation. With the UI Path Community Edition, business teams, analysts, and developers can begin experimenting creating RPA scripts without a full enterprise platform commitment.

Create Value-Added Robots and Robot Evangelists

As companies experiment with these robots, they should begin creating robots that add value to their organizations. This is the true beginning of the RPA journey and the true beginning of identifying organizational change management requirements as robots are deployed.

Robot evangelists should also be identified within the organization responsible for tracking productivity gains created by deploying robots in addition to identifying organizational change management initiatives required to support new robotic workers.

Identify Structured Data Solutions

One of the primary benefits of an RPA solution is that it can leverage your existing systems and existing business processes for automation but these solutions require structured data to be successful out of the box.

Excellent initial use cases for RPA focus on a highly manual process that interact with multiple systems for data entry and processing. Most RPA platforms (without integration to packaged or custom natural language processing systems) work best when the data is structured for data entry and processing and can be enhanced with basic business rules to make decisions and execute business processes.

By identifying structured data solutions, teams can quickly identify quick win projects with immediate ROI as Tier 1 projects, identify value-added AI integrations as Tier 2 projects, and identify the beginnings of an enterprise automation roadmap.

Create an Enterprise Automation Roadmap (EAR)

Creating an EAR focuses on understanding the manual processes that are currently being supported, identifying which processes can be automated where re-keying and data re-entry occur and then identify solutions that can be used to solve this problem. It's important to note that one tool can't solve every unautomated problem in an organization.

The EAR should focus on how robotic process automation should be used and the primary goals. EARs can define organization goals such as:

- Automated integration management
- Human Capital Productivity Improvements
- Full Robotic Automation projects
- Quality Improvement projects
- Stepping-stone for other IT deployments

RPA solutions may be deployed where the process isn't fully automated but have some human supervision to manage exceptions. As exceptions are catalogued and resolved, this information can be integrated into the RPA processes to enhance and reduce exceptions over time.

Enterprise Communication and Change Management

Employees see RPA as a threat to their jobs, however, in most instances RPA deployments haven't caused terminations in companies, but instead resulted in redeployments of employees to higher-valued positions. Companies that position an RPA deployments as an 'assistant' to the human find better results in their implementations.

Because many corporate executives see a threat that their headcount may be replaced with robots, some companies will have challenges in getting alignment across the organization for RPA deployments.

Getting alignment with an EAR strategy can help to manage stakeholders as their departments and processes become integrated to highly automated machines.

Create a Center of Excellence (COE)

Van states that RPA automation excels when supported by a COE. A COE consists of a process funnel manager who helps to prioritize requests, documentation processes to identify robot tasks and requirements, developers who specialize in RPA scripting. Van states that this unit should sit closer to business units instead of IT. This can optimize the throughput and domain knowledge of the COE and improve productivity within the COE since reusable libraries of automations can be created and managed.

Internal Training and Supervision

Many RPA implementations begin with quick-win proof of conceptd, but when the consultants leave, a good RPA process requires supervision, support and training. Common issues occur because of data quality from upstream inputs that lead to unexpected errors, or due to changes that occur with systems over time.

RPA can be used to automate organizational processes including back office functions such as procurement, financial functions such as invoice processing, data lookup functions such as manufacturer sku lookups and descriptions, software testing automation, competitor analysis and reporting, and claims processing. There's no limit to what RPA can accomplish. If there's a screen, some data, and a process RPA is flexible enough to handle many unique processes.

HR Process Integration

At the point of true RPA adoption, HR teams become integral to identifying automation opportunities. As attrition occurs within an organization, HR teams should evaluate open job descriptions and identify if the headcount should be replaced by a new hire or replaced by a robot.

These assessments may occur not only at an individual position level, but also within a department. If a robot can automate 20% of the activities on a team of 5 people, then entire departments may be restructured as a result.

There are tremendous implications for Learning and Development teams in planning for RPA rollouts. L&D teams need to restructure their responsibilities to create development and training plans to increase the skills of their employees.

RPA Solution Maturity

RPA projects should be implemented in phases combined with quick wins as well as strategic integrations to AI systems managed as part of the roadmap.

Most companies using RPA today are using a hard-coded rules engine for back office processing, but with new investments in AI technologies, RPA is going to become better as AI technologies improve.

Like AI, RPA is also an evolution. Most companies have a capability maturity model regarding how they implement technology and RPA is no exception. There are 4 different levels to RPA maturity within projects.

Application Automation

Companies in the application automation stage focus on automating a single business process in a single application. This could be done through a pure automation or could be done though a robot assistant- a robot that interacts with a user to augment a function performed by a person either manually or automatically.

Typically, applications in this state have hard-coded business rules and macro automations and interact with a single application or within a BPM process.

User Interaction Automation

User automation involves automations that automate and mimic actual user activity and business rules across one or more systems. This is done through either pure automation, or could also be integrated through a robot assistant.

Applications that automate user interactions can support more complex workflows, creating/updating data across multiple systems in multiple platforms, and can work within legacy applications. These applications typically have some level of hard-coded rules and workflows.

Cognitive Robot Automation

Cognitive Robot Automation integrates basic cognitive services such as computer vision, OCR, and natural language processing to create smarter robots that 'do more'. An organization will evolve from User Interaction Automation processes for the initial version of the process, then escalate exceptions to human workers to process. From there, cognitive services are introduced once training data is gathered from the manual escalation processes and incorporated into the robot processes.

AI Robots

AI robots are the final level of robot complexity and sophistication in an organization. These robots will have the ability to be 'trained' by humans but also have access to massive amounts of data to make real-time decisions optimized for your business. This level of AI performs as well (and in most cases better) than people in roles within an organization.

Potential Problems

Problems arise in every project and RPA is no exception. Van states that many RPA projects over-promise and under-deliver. It's important to manage expectations on what RPA does and does not do. The second major risk area is around organizational change management and the communication plan related to a robot rollout.

Most organizations implementing RPA do not cut staff because of RPA, but instead focus on redeploying employees to handle new assignments that add higher value to an organization.

In one of the case studies covered later in the book, JP Morgan deployed a robot/AI solution that completed 360,000 hours in minutes. People were redeployed in the organization instead of laid off.

As of this writing, there is only one reported incident on Glassdoor.com reporting their position was replaced by a robot. With proper change management and organizational planning, it's easy to avoid this situation.

Vendor Selection

Van states that vendor selection is a major problem in the RPA industry. Van states that there are several companies who are positioning themselves as experts who are not.

For companies that choose to go it alone, he recommends bringing in a third-party implementer who has experience in more than one RPA solution to help with initial deployments for RPA.

He also cites that lack of organizational change management can create problems for robot rollouts and the lack of a COE to be key factors in robot rollout and adoption. Van recommends that companies plan for a COE to manage robot projects since there is typically an influx in demand once the technology is available in the organization.

Payback Timeframe

In most cases, RPA can handle the workload of 3-10 FTEs at approximately 10-20% of the cost. Van estimates that in most business processes there is a 4 to 1 ratio of productivity when robots are deployed (1 robot for 4 employees.)

It's estimated that 60-80% of structured business processes can be automated using RPA and that even processes that aren't used frequently can be automated with a positive net value.

The average payback of an RPA project is 3-9 months and solutions can be implemented in production in just a few weeks. Because an RPA solution uses existing systems and business processes, it's easy to deploy your new robot army and subsequently increase your robot workforce based on your needs and as exceptions to standard processes get catalogued and managed[4].

The Future of RPA

RPA vendors are focused on adding more AI capabilities natively into their platforms. RPA platforms already support integrations into AI platforms such as Watson or OCR libraries but RPA companies are also integrating their own AI into their platforms to expand the functionality without adding new infrastructure.

Van states that the next generation of RPA solutions will be self-generating. By recording employees keystrokes and application usage, robots will be able to be automatically created without the steps today for recording and scripting robots.

RPA solutions have less than a 10% market saturation which creates huge opportunities for companies to make technology investments that create real ROI and dramatically improve corporate productivity.

If your competitors are implementing RPA, your company is at risk of being outmanned by their robot army and outgunned with new innovative processes created by teams with new capacity created by automation.

Imagine having 10-20% more capacity across your teams by implementing RPA automation. That is what RPA can do.

Notes

[1] https://willrobotstakemyjob.com

[2] http://www.oxfordmartin.ox.ac.uk/downloads/academic/The_Future_of_Employment.pdf

[3] https://www.edgeverve.com/wp-content/uploads/2017/02/forrester-wave-robotic-process-automation.pdf

[4] http://www.roboticstomorrow.com/article/2016/07/the-abc-of-rpa-part-5-what-is-the-cost-of-automation-and-how-do-i-justify-it-to-the-leadership-team/8483/

CHAPTER 4

Machine Learning

Machine learning is usually one of the first AI algorithms deployed within an organization. Machine learning is also sometimes referred to as predictive analytics, which is the ability to use past data to predict the future.

The way that these algorithms work is through a probability assessment based on the historical data provided. Models are created by analyzing past data and determining the statistical relevance of a variable.

Creating a Model

Here are the steps that data scientists follow to create and deploy a machine learning model:

1. Problem Identification
2. Data Cleansing
3. Model Identification
4. Model Training
5. Deployment

Problem Identification

When you hire a data scientist, the first question they are going to ask is what type of insights are you looking for from your data. This is a crucial step in identifying what type of algorithms to use and what data to evaluate. Most machine learning algorithms are designed to do a few things:

Classification is used to identify a set of categories that the data belongs to. It's primarily used to predict a category. Examples of classification could be customer segmentation, identify product categories, or identify specific customer attributes.

Clustering is like classification but with a slight difference. In Classification, you have a known set of variables (age, zip code, gender, etc). In clustering, you have unknown variables that are used do things such as create customer segments, predict consumer tastes, and determine market prices for products.

Regression is used to predict a number or probability of an outcome. Regression analysis can be used to estimate product demand, create sales forecasts, and analyze returns on project investments.

Anomaly Detection is used to identify anomalies with data. Examples of this include things like detecting fraud, identify malfunctioning equipment, identifying 'hacker' traffic on your network.

The two most common algorithms used are classification and regression.

Data Cleansing

Data cleansing occurs to prepare the data for training. This includes a number of steps such as replacing blank values with information (data scientists often use averages for blank values so the data analysis isn't skewed). Machine learning algorithms also don't tend to do well with text-based categories, so many algorithms require you to transform the data from text-based categories into numeric categories. Data cleansing projects also typically require pulling information from multiple data sources and combining these together into one set of data for analysis.

Model Identification

Model identification is very much dependent on the types of answers you are looking for. This will depend on whether you use a regression algorithm or a classification algorithm. The type of data you have will depend on which algorithm you choose.

Data scientists test multiple algorithms for a problem to determine which one produces the most accurate results and verify that the results meet intuitively with what the problem is expected to answer. They perform several tests looking for overfitting, a scenario in which the test data and training data are so similar that high accuracy is seen in the results, but doesn't represent what would happen with real data.

Model Training

Model training occurs by using historical data to 'train a model.' This training occurs by segmenting a test set of data with a training set of data (usually 80% of data is used for training, then the model is tested with 20% of the data – depending on the number of records.)

During the training phase data is chosen at random between test and train. Once the model is trained, then the test data is passed into the model and the results are compared to the actual results.

When training a model, models that are less than 60% accurate are no better than guessing. Models with 60-70% accuracy are considered poor. Models with 70-80% accuracy are considered good. Models with 80-90% accuracy are very good. Models that have over 90% accuracy are considered 'too good' meaning that the test data likely has a problem with overfitting.

Deployment

Once a model is created, tested, trained and analyzed, the next step is deployment. Often companies will deploy a model side-by-side to the current process so that the results can be analyzed without disruption to existing business processes.

Because these are math formulas, there is no such thing as a crystal ball and this must be considered when rolling out machine learning. There is a second level of analysis that should be completed based on financial modeling of different decisions.

For example, if you deploy a customer retention campaign that offers a $10 discount off their next purchase, financial models should be created that estimate the number of 'false positive' records that would get the offer. In this example, a machine-learning based campaign would send the offer to both customers who were a one-time customer (the target group) and customers who were a repeat customer (the false positives). In current machine learning standards, you could expect 20% of your customers to get the offer even though they weren't part of your target group.

Once you've deployed your model, you may not be done. Machine learning algorithms may need to be re-trained as your data and customer demographics change.

It's important to define a process to review the ML accuracy on a regular basis.

Examples

An example of machine learning algorithms would be in the case of estimating a credit score: the algorithm would evaluate the credit payment history of a person, their salary, gender, their work history, their home ownership status, their outstanding debt, their zip code and other information to create a math formula to predict a credit score.

Financial sectors were early adopters of machine learning so the real models are undoubtedly more complex than this, however - initially when credit scores were created they probably were very similar with hard-coded business rules.

The summary is machine learning creates math formulas based on historical data and can be retrained over time as more data is added.

A different example would be a salary recommendation system that evaluates a person's resume and then recommends an offer for that person to join your company.

This brings up another problem with machine learning algorithms is having a problem with bias.

Bias in Machine Learning

Bias is a term used in Machine Learning when the data used to create the model can influence the predictions it makes. This is also called the Bias/Variance Tradeoff – where very similar data creates predictable outcomes. With variance (or highly varied data), you need a lot of data to create a meaningful prediction.

Bias comes from a couple different sources - one area comes from under-representation of data. This means that when the computer sees new data, it doesn't know how to handle it because it hasn't seen that situation before.

A second scenario occurs because the dataset already contains a bias within the data. This means that new information sent into an algorithm will categorize it based on similar past data - but it may not produce the results that you want.

In an under-representation example, I had created a mobile app that used Microsoft Cognitive APIs to perform facial recognition. When our team tested the app and facial recognition, it worked perfectly. I then tested the app with my very dark-skinned friend and the app couldn't identify her at all. Pokémon Go also had a similar experience, where players in primarily black neighborhoods saw fewer Pokémon locations. This occurred because the software developers weren't spending time in those neighborhoods[1].

A famous case of data-centric bias occurred on LinkedIn[1]. LinkedIn had algorithms that were displaying ads for jobs. For LinkedIn's female audience, the ads targeted to them were for lower-paying jobs than the ads displayed for men. In this scenario, LinkedIn's algorithms were promoting the bias - making the machine learning algorithms even stronger and even reinforcing the behavior that women should be paid less than their male peers.

In March of 2016, Microsoft created a chatbot on Twitter called Tay.ai that within 24 hours became a Nazi-loving racist[2]. With the Tay example, they had modeled Tay to interact with 18-24 year olds and mimic their behavior.

What happened is that many internet trolls trained Tay to repeat inappropriate comments.

"This was to be expected," said Roman Yampolskiy, head of the CyberSecurity lab at the University of Louisville, who has published a paper about pathways to dangerous AI. "The system is designed to learn from its users, so it will become a reflection of their behavior," he said. "One needs to explicitly teach a system about what is not appropriate, like we do with children."[2]

Zip codes are often a source of data bias since they tend to be a very accurate representation of income levels and socioeconomic status in a community.

In these types of instances, bias rules should be *created* to handle biased data so the machine can be trained to learn 'right' from 'wrong'.

Notes

[1] http://www.techrepublic.com/article/bias-in-machine-learning-and-how-to-stop-it/

[1] http://www.techrepublic.com/article/why-microsofts-tay-ai-bot-went-wrong/

CHAPTER 5

Deep Learning

If machine learning is the foundation of AI, Deep Learning is the more sophisticated cousin of machine learning and is at the heart of the most complex AI algorithms in the world.

Deep Learning is a set of algorithms that arrange data in layers. It's modeled after the way that a human mind works. Neurons work together to piece together information and then combine the information to make a prediction, deciding from the data what's important and what is not.

A Deep Learning neural network works in a similar way. Data is passed into the network. A pattern is identified in the network and the data is weighted based on the relevance to the output or prediction. Multiple levels of networks can be created, each recognizing patterns within the patterns to predict an outcome.

Most Deep Learning solutions are implemented using one of the frameworks previously discussed (Tensorflow, Torch, Keras, Theano).

The biggest challenge around deep learning projects is that it takes significantly more data to train, it takes longer to train, and requires more processing power for performance than a machine learning solution requires.

However, the biggest advantage that deep learning provides is that you can build highly sophisticated models that learn and change over time.

Examples

Deep Learning is used in multiple AI disciplines such as computer vision and natural language processing.

Deep Learning was used to create a 9-minute screenplay[1] that was created by analyzing the scripts of dozens of science fiction movies including Highlander and The Fifth Element. The verdict was that "screenwriters have nothing to fear" but the fact that an AI created a new and original script is an amazing start.

Most Deep Learning solutions focus on categorizing and analyzing unstructured data such as image recognition, documentation, anomaly detection and video detection.

Kaggle.com[2] is a site that supports machine learning and deep learning enthusiasts by providing high quality data sets for learning purposes. They also host competitions where companies such as Zillow provide a prize to competitors who can improve Zillow's home value prediction algorithms.

At the time of this writing, the US Department of Homeland Security has a $1.5m prize to improve the accuracy of the passenger screening algorithms. Developers in Kaggle competitions even post links to their source code for their solutions in sites such as Github, a popular code repository.

Adobe uses Deep Learning in their platform to help designers identify fonts that are being used based on data from a 20,000 font database. Pinterest[3] created a visual search tool using Caffe to identify specific products within one of their pictures.

For example, a Pinterest user can zoom in on a photo of a lamp in a room, then identify pins of similar items and where to purchase it.

Handwriting recognition is another example of how deep learning platforms can be used to create structured data out of unstructured data.

Problems

One of the bigger problems of Deep Learning is getting good classifications of data. Deep Learning requires high quality data and, depending on the accuracy of your source this can be expensive to get.

Dr. Igor Barani, former CEO of Enlitic which is an AI company focused on medical screening solutions, stated that the biggest challenges to companies is "Finding the right problem, getting the right data, and getting enough data." He described some challenges with a screening solution for radiology to detect abnormal results in lung screenings.

During the project, the team found that of the three radiology experts assigned to the team, they only agreed on a diagnosis 40% of the time – leading to major questions regarding the integrity of the data and the results they would get at the end of the project.

Another major issue with deep learning is that it's not always clear how the results of the algorithm were derived. With machine learning it's easy to see what data points fall into the chart. Because deep learning can have hundreds of layers of information, it's not always intuitive as to how the answer was derived by the computer.

Deep Learning also requires GPU processors to be performant, making it very expensive to process data comparatively to machine learning solutions which can be implemented on standard open source servers.

For companies looking to evolve their corporate intelligence, Deep Learning provides the next logical stepping stone to creating highly efficient and accurate algorithms for data processing and analysis.

Notes

[1] https://arstechnica.com/gaming/2016/06/an-ai-wrote-this-movie-and-its-strangely-moving/

[2] https://www.kaggle.com/competitions

[3] https://news.developer.nvidia.com/pinterest-sharpens-its-visual-search-skills/

CHAPTER 6

Chatbots/Virtual Agents

Many companies will begin their AI journey starting with Chatbots or Virtual Agents. There are a several types of Chatbots in the market available today, ranging from text-based agents to voice-based agents.

Choosing your interface and platform for Chatbots and virtual agents vary based on your target market and the services you provide.

The key advantage of using a Chatbot over creating an app for customer interactions and notifications is the ability to integrate into other apps that the user uses daily.

Forrester reports that 80% of apps that are downloaded are deleted after their first use and people spend 84% of their time in only 5 apps[1]. For many cases, it makes a lot of sense to integrate into one of those five apps instead of becoming one of the 80% of deleted apps.

A Chatbot gives you the capability to interact with your customers through existing social channels and gain new ways to engage with your customers on the platforms they frequent.

Within the bot space, there are several different types of bots you can deploy based on your target market and use case.

Superbots

Superbots are platforms such as Amazon Alexa, Siri, Microsoft Cortana, and Google Assistant. These platforms have invested money and time in creating developer communities to integrate to their solutions. At this time, the current leading superbot is Alexa who supports over 15,000 commands. As of June 2017, Alexa has 15,069 skills, Google Assistant 378 while Microsoft Cortana has 65[2]. Apple's number of Siri commands is currently unpublished.

The good part about these superbots is that they make it easy to "do something" and can span across multiple domains. Use Slack to order an Uber. Use Alexa to order a Domino's Pizza. The span of what these bots can do is vast.

The bad part of these superbots is (much like domain names) that the good commands are taken. If you want to recommend wines, a winebot is already in play. If you want to track your goals, it's done. It's also a single-channel solution. You can't ask Cortana to add items to your Amazon shopping list in preparation for an upcoming meeting on your calendar.

Voice-based solutions also can be clunky when designed poorly. Amazon's open the magic door command is a choose your own adventure type of game targeted toward children. In the magic door game, it constantly repeats what you just said at a slow pace, making it an infuriatingly annoying for anyone over the age of three.

If your company has a B2C play and wants to be able to interact with your users through voice and create real value, these superbots can do it once you program your skill and integrate into the superbot ecosystem.

Shopping Bots

Shopping bots can take several forms. There are Shopping Bot platforms that are designed to aggregate information from multiple shopping websites and show end users products they may be interested in. Shopping bots can also be created by individual companies showcasing their own products.

Kip is a shopping chatbot that is targeted toward teenagers. Kip supports 80 different merchant feeds in their shopping bot which enables users to search for products in one place and check out automatically using Kip.

Individual companies can create their own bot interfaces and integrate to platforms such as Facebook and WhatsApp to promote their products. H&M created a chatbot that shows their primarily teen audience new looks and deals and allows them to buy directly through their bot. H&M created their chatbot on Kik, a messaging platform targeted towards teens that currently has half a million users.

Amtrak implemented a chatbot called Julie which allows customers to book train tickets online[3]. When Amtrack implemented Julie, the result was some very impressive metrics:

- 25% more bookings
- $1M in customer service costs saved
- 50% YOY growth in engagement with Julye
- 30% more revenue per booking

Business Bots

Slack

Slack has several bot integrations - everything from scheduling an Uber or Lyft to ordering office supplies to automating daily status meetings for teams. Slack bots work by installing a bot to the Slack team, then depending on the bot's purpose (is a team bot or a personal bot) will either publish information in a Slack channel, will message someone directly, or interface with a third-party service.

Many Slack bots work through a command-line interface, making them more challenging for people to learn how to create an action using a bot.

For example, to call an Uber a user types in /uber ride [from address] to [to address]

This command requests an Uber and sends it to your location. You can use similar commands to request status updates of your Uber or get price estimates.

App-based bots

When apps came out, it was a very conscientious startup strategy to say if you are an App-first startup or a Web-first startup. With AI-powered technologies, startups may opt for a third choice: the bot-first startup.

Poncho

Poncho is a bot that delivers a daily weather report - with an attitude. Poncho has a frontend that allows you to customize the type of daily notifications you get (such as the weather, potential traffic issues, in addition to fun information such as whether it's a bad hair day). Poncho also has an AI backend that customizes your notifications based on your interactions with Poncho.

Using Bots for Your Business

Bots can not only be deployed to engage with your customers, but they can also be deployed and integrated into your current business processes to improve your capabilities and productivity.

Amy

Amy (X.ai) is a virtual assistant that schedules meetings for you. By CCing Amy on a meeting request, she can send emails to multiple people and arrange times, dates, and locations for a meeting.

Amy uses natural language processing coupled with multiple deep learning algorithms to coordinate times, set up the location (either in person or a conference call), follow-up on outstanding meeting requests, then ultimately create the invitation and update meetings when necessary.

Amy is often seen as a real assistant so be forewarned. When scheduling meetings I've found that Amy isn't 100% accurate and even when I point out that she's 'an AI assistant', the AI part is often missed and when Amy makes a mistake – people get very confused.

Cortana

Cortana is Microsoft's AI assistant integrated into the Windows 10 platform. Cortana can be used to view your calendar appointments, get news updates, play music, set reminders, or search the internet. Cortana can be customized to automate business functions.

What if your company had a competitive dashboard that could be accessed through Cortana. Say 'show me the competitive dashboard' and Cortana would look up the following:

1. Your stock price compared to your competitors
2. A summary of blog articles or news articles published in your industry within the past 24 hours
3. A summary of your company's social feeds (including the number of followers and sentiments in the last 24 hours)
4. And then Cortana (or any bot really) can take the next step to send the relevant information to the right department for review and analysis

Now that's a game changer.

Chatbot Development Platforms

Chatbot development platforms vary from custom-coded solutions using APIs and SDKs to bot platforms that can be configured. We'll cover a few of the leading platforms and some of the scenarios they handle.

Chatfuel

Chatfuel is the leading bot developer for Facebook and Telegram. They have made it easy to deploy a bot to these platforms with just a few clicks. Chatfuel provides pre-packaged interfaces that can be used to customize your scripts.

Chatfuel is designed for non-developers to implement chat programs with standard interfaces pre-designed. Chatfuel integrates to several different third-party systems and can be integrated into custom APIs for added capabilities.

Chatfuel allows you to easily broadcast messages, capture users based on Facebook interactions, and gives you reporting capabilities to measure engagement. They currently have 46,000 customers and have a free version available.

FlowXO

FlowXO is a development platform that supports multiple integrations including Facebook, Slack, Telegram, Twilio (for text-messaging integration), and Web.

FlowXO also is a code-free platform where you can create chat scripts and allows you to connect to third party API services for additional information. FlowXO makes it easy to create conversation flowcharts that perform pattern matching to identify the conversation context.

For example, you can create a conversation flow that identifies if a person landing on your website is a new customer or existing customer, and then branch off to scripts targeted toward those individual user types.

Botkit.AI

Botkit is an open source bot toolkit that enables you to build bots for free using their platform which integrates to third-party platforms including Slack, Facebook, Watson, Twilio.

Botkit provides starter projects for the major platforms that enable you to get your bot up and running quickly. Botkit offers APIs connected to their Botkit studio platform and can be easily integrated with web applications using Node.js.

Microsoft Bot Framework

The Microsoft Bot framework is a Microsoft-based framework that integrates easily to other services such as LUIS, Microsoft's natural language interpreter platform that dissects a user request and determines an action associated to it making it easier to determine conversation flow in a bot.

Microsoft also supports many integrations including Facebook, Slack, Skype, Cortana, Alexa, Kik, Skype and others. Microsoft's bot framework is coded using Node.js or C#.

Microsoft has also developed APIs to store conversation data, save the context of the conversation with a specific user, and create custom integrations from your own platforms into their bot framework.

IBM Watson

IBM Watson provides a no-coding interface to create a chatbot script which enables you to plug into Watson's capabilities such as natural language processing, natural language understanding, and sentiment analysis. Deploying a Watson chatbot to a platform requires development using Node.js. Watson also provides a Virtual Agent services that is pre-trained to answer common questions for many industries.

The interesting thing about the chatbot and virtual agent market is that they are interoperable. You can create a chatbot on Chatfuel that calls the Microsoft language understanding framework (LUIS), which then calls the Watson sentiment analysis framework and then ends up displaying an emoticon or special offer based on information derived from these sources all provided by services on the cloud.

Implementing Bots in Your Organization

Creating a bot within your organization (either for internal or external use) requires some planning and doesn't follow a typical software implementation project plan because there are several unknowns relative to how people interact with your bot.

With the bot revolution happening, it's important to design a bot experience that meets people's expectations. Today these expectations are relatively low, so this is a new area where you can 'surprise and delight' your customers by creating innovative bots that provide useful services and information to your users.

Here are some things to consider as you are starting on your bot journey.

Audience

Selecting your audience and use case is the first step in your bot design. This is the primary criteria for the rest of the decisions relative to your bot. What demographics are you targeting? How is your bot going to be used? To showcase new products or engage with your customers? What are the goals of your bot? To create new leads for your business or to assist with pre-sales questions? Does your bot automate a business process? These are the decisions that set the foundation for your bot.

Engagement

How does a user interact with your bot?

The goal of your bot should focus on creating a great first impression and then adding enough value that creates a habit to use your bot on a regular basis.

With the lessons learned from the app market, companies created apps to engage with their customers, but the companies with the *best* apps created incentives for their users to continue using the app.

A bot gives you a new and novel interface to engage with your customers, but it needs to be unique enough and add enough value for the user to adopt the bot and not get frustrated and annoyed with the experience.

Personality

Your bot is a representation and extension of your brand. It needs to reflect the voice and personality of your brand.

When X.ai created Amy, the email bot that schedules meetings, they invested a large quantity of time determining how Amy should talk to people. They developed a script based on an ideal personal assistant – polite, friendly, professional, and clear.

A bot can be the first impression of your brand and by designing a bot with these design attributes first, they were able to create a useful bot that, while Amy doesn't pass the Turing test, is useful for hundreds of thousands of users saving them millions of hours of meeting scheduling ping-poing.

Platform

Selecting the platform for your bot is based on your use case and your target market. If you are designing a B2C bot, using Facebook or Kik (a messaging platform for teens) might be the right platform for your bot.

If you have products that are sold online, an Alexa or Google skill which creates voice to text capabilities may be the way to enter the bot-o-sphere. If you target B2B customers, many companies integrate to Slack to provide useful services.

The easiest way to test the waters of bot development is to use solutions like Flowxo or Chatfuel to create website plugins for sales and service.

Other ways to explore bot development are to leverage solutions like Microsoft's bot framework or an open source framework like Botkit. These solutions give you one platform for multiple channels, although some work is needed to customize your content for those channels.

Personal Vs. Team

A large part of determining your design of your bot is to determine how your bot is going to interact with people. Is it targeted toward a person or is it targeted for a group of people?

For bots that automate business processes, designing a bot based on the context of a conversation from one person has very different design considerations than bots that facilitate team activities.

Name and Brand

Creating a name for your bot inherently gives your bot a personality and humanizes your bot. Creating the branding to support your bot makes it recognizable among a sea of other bots.

This includes not only a name for your bot but the colors, the branding, the logo, and images that can be used with communications to your customers.

Log Monitoring

Most bots are designed using keyword matching algorithms (although some AI-based Chatbots are coming onto the market.)

With these types of solutions, people typically know they are talking to a bot and a few things happen.

1. The customer may get frustrated with the experience.
2. The customer tries to mess with the bot.
3. The bot gets 'lost' along the way and doesn't understand the context of the conversation anymore.

By reviewing your logs regularly, you can identify common requests from users making it easier for them to interact with your bot. You can identify patterns of conversations that end with a bad user experience and you can learn how to elegantly handle unexpected text inputs by guiding people to the right solution.

Escalation

An escalation process is a crucial part of bot design, particularly in the early stages of implementation when you haven't learned how people are interacting with your bot.

Having a human escalation process may be crucial depending on your target audience. If you have a customer service help bot, you will likely be able to solve up to 40% of your incidents using a bot for FAQs and common help requests.

But if there isn't an escalation process built in for the other 60% of the cases, you'll leave your customers frustrated and annoyed with you and your company.

Onboarding

Today's bots can be dumb and most of the bot platforms are not currently integrated with AI. Most bot implementations focus on keyword matching and converse based on matching keywords to create a response to a customer request.

For bots to be effective today, they should train their users on how to use them. For many of the 'super-bots' (Alexa, Google Home, Cortana) this is going to become a huge challenge as the number of skills in those platforms grow.

Today Alexa supports over 15,000 commands and has grown exponentially over the course of the past two years since rolling out their product.

Companies that invest in training their users how to use their bot will see higher adoption rates.

For onboarding, X.Ai's Amy sends several emails to you letting you know how she responds to commands, verifying updates to your account information, and providing guidance when she doesn't understand what you said.

She also provides an escalation email for you to send feedback to a person to review your communication with Amy and work through issues.

Analytics

There are two parts of creating analytics: the first of which is defining the success metrics and the second of which is the measurements. With apps, vanity metrics were created based on number of app downloads. These vanity metrics defined success, but didn't really measure success. Your analytics should include things like click-through rates, purchases, positive and negative sentiments, number of engagement and repeated engagement.

By performing these steps you can have a successful bot implementation that adds a lot of value to your organization.

Notes

[1] http://www.techrepublic.com/article/your-app-strategy-is-probably-going-to-fail-heres-how-to-fix-it/

[2] https://www.voicebot.ai/2017/07/02/amazon-alexa-skill-count-passes-15000-in-the-u-s/

[3] http://www.businesswire.com/news/home/20160120005909/en/Intelligent-Assistant-Amtrak-Wins-Global-Award-Consumer

CHAPTER 7

Computer Vision

Computer vision is a growing area in AI development. Computer vision allows a computer to process information from an image as part of a workflow process.
Some applications of computer vision include:

- Reading emotions from people's faces during product testing sessions to document sentiments
- Search for similar images
- Facial detection and recognition
- Medical image analytics
- Object Recognition
- Optical Character Recognition (OCR)
- Handwriting Recognition
- Augmented Reality

Several companies offer specialized computer vision services in addition to the major tech companies. Blogger Gaurav Oberoi[1] performed a test on the major image processing APIs including Microsoft, Google, IBM, Cloudsight, Clarifai.

His test focused on image labeling accuracy across these vendors and here's what he found:

- Most images were labeled correctly with their top-level category
- Most image processors labeled the entire picture contents, not necessarily just the focus element
- Some image processors combine both machine learning with crowd sourcing technologies to label images. One vendor in particular, Cloudsight, was sent the same image multiple times and came back with different labels - suggesting a human-based label instead of automated label.
- Images require the right orientation to be analyzed correctly. Inaccuracy was very high when an image was submitted upside-down.
- He found that Clarifai had the best results, followed by Google then Microsoft.
- Images cropped to focus on the 'area of interest' had a high degree of accuracy

Computer Vision Technologies

OpenCV

OpenCV is an open source library that has libraries available for Python, C++, Java and IOS. OpenCV provides several services including facial recognition, object tracking, image stitching, and image processing libraries.

Using these libraries often take more coding to implement than using professional services and libraries.

Microsoft Computer Vision APIs

As part of their Cognitive Services suite of tools, Microsoft offers computer vision APIs hosted on their Azure platform which provides services ranging from image labeling to facial recognition to age classification to OCR capabilities.

Microsoft offers an API that is easy to implement that supports either an image uploaded to their servers or through a URL.

Google Computer Vision API

As part of their Google Cloud offering, Google offers a computer vision API that includes capabilities such as safe image searching (categorizing for inappropriate content), facial detection, celebrity recognition, landmark detection, and text detection. Facial recognition is not supported by Google apis.

IBM Watson

IBM Watson provides image recognition capabilities such as classification, facial recognition, similar image searching, and allows you to create your own image classification models.

AWS Rekognition

AWS provides Deep Learning-based APIs that provide capabilities such as facial recognition, object labeling, image moderation, facial analysis, and celebrity recognition services.

Clarifai

Clarifai provides image processing capabilities on their cloud platform including image categorization, image search similarity, moderation, and allows you to create your own image classification models for specialized applications.

Deep Learning Technologies

Deep learning algorithms such as Artificial Neural Networks (ANN) and Convolutional Neural Networks (CNN) can be used to create machine learning models for computer vision capabilities.

Tensorflow's ANN and CNN algorithms can also be used to create these models. These algorithms work by training a model based using images that have already been classified.

ANN is used in applications including image classification, natural language processing, and statistical probability uses. ANNs work by taking an input (in this scenario, an image), getting the output (which could be a label), then creating a 'hidden layer' to classify features of the image.

For example, if training an image classification based on a set of dog images versus cat images, an ANN algorithm would take a set of images that were classified as dogs and cats and then identify features associated to dogs and cats, then weight them appropriately to define a model that predicts whether the image is a dog or a cat.

With CNN algorithms, an image is sliced up into smaller segments multiple times, then a value is calculated for that segment. That value is weighted among similar results to figure out the right answer.

Within organizations, the two most challenging AI technologies to implement are computer vision and natural language processing.

Examples

Sunglass Hut implemented a 'My Frame Finder' functionality which allows users to quickly see other sunglass frame styles that are based on similar features to a selected category.

Historically ecommerce systems would tag images within a category and would use that category to show similar images. These all required a manual process to create the categories and apply the appropriate categories to the image. With computer vision, you can identify similar styles to a selected pair of sunglasses without the human component.

Similar functionality could be used for identifying designer outfits and finding similar styles at other retailers to 'create the look' at any budget.

Notes

[1] https://goberoi.com/comparing-the-top-five-computer-vision-apis-98e3e3d7c647

CHAPTER 8

Natural Language Processing

Natural language processing is an area of AI focused on two distinct capabilities:

- Natural Language Understanding: the capability of a computer to understand a person
- Natural Language Generation: the capability of a computer to speak like a person

There are several challenges with implementing natural language processing within most organizations. The most advanced commercial APIs in this space focus on interpreting natural language to create actions and objects.

For example, a request to track exercise in a fitness app could be said in multiple ways:

- I went swimming
- I am running
- I went for a jog
- I can't run. I hurt my !@#$ knee.

As a human, we know a lot of things about these 4 statements:

- Swimming is different than running
- Running and jogging are probably the same thing
- The person who hurt their knee is unhappy (sentiment analysis) and I probably shouldn't ask them tomorrow if they went running otherwise I might annoy them.

The biggest challenge around natural language processing is that the language is VERY context specific. There's very different language used by a lawyer versus a doctor, and creating the rules around the language (called a corpus) is necessary to get accurate NLP results.

NLP Solutions

Deep Learning

Deep Learning Neural Networks can be used to create natural language processing solutions. There are dozens of different deep learning algorithms that can be used to create NLP solutions.

Technologies such as Tensorflow and Torch can be used for classification of language. Technologies such as LSTM (Long Short Term Memory – a type of deep learning algorithm) can be used to create sentiment analysis.

Microsoft LUIS

Microsoft LUIS makes it faster to integrate NLP into your applications. There are four key elements to begin creating your LUIS application:

1. Creating a list of intents, actions that you would expect a user to ask for.
2. Create entities associated to the intent.
3. Define features which are possible values for the entities.
4. Provide patterns which can be used by LUIS to determine features as well.

An example of how NLP could be deployed would be for an airline reservations bot.

1. A few intents for this app might be 'book a flight', 'get prices', 'reschedule a flight'
2. Some entities would be Departure City, Destination City, departure date, return date, ticket number.
3. A feature would be a list of cities that the airline supports or if the flight is direct or non-stop.
4. A pattern might be the pattern of the reservation number. If someone enters in ticket 545EA58bh3, LUIS could identify that's most likely a ticket number and ask questions related to an existing ticket (instead of booking a new flight.)

LUIS would take the text and try to find a match for one of the possible intents, the entity values for the intent, and the probability of a match.

IBM Watson

Watson provides several different products focused on NLP including Conversation (for chatbot interfaces), documentation conversion which is used to take organizational documents and convert to multiple languages and file types.

Watson provides a Natural Language Understanding service that is used to extract concepts, keywords, categories, and sentiment from text. Watson also provides text to speech and speech to text capabilities.

Google Cloud Natural Language API

Google's API provides a detailed analysis of a sentence passed into its API. It can be used to identify intent, understand sentiment, and extract information such as people, places events and more. The Google Cloud Natural Language api provides entities, sentiments and a structured breakdown of a sentences as shown below:

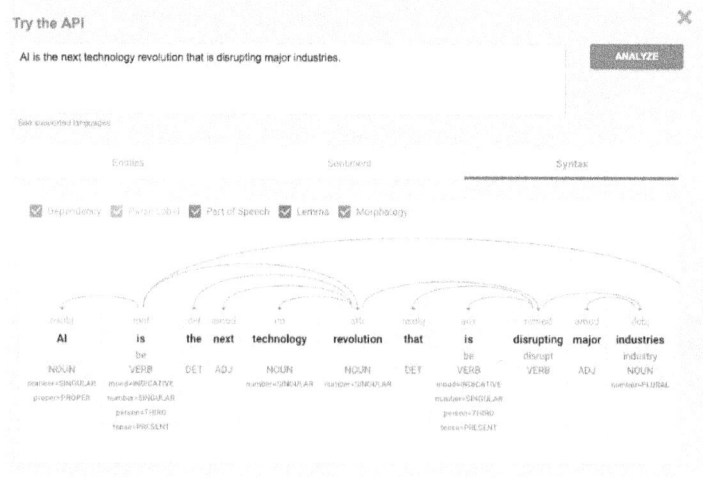

Source: Google Cloud Natural Language API[1]

Amazon Lex

Amazon Lex provides the same technologies that support Amazon's Alexa platform. Lex supports both speech recognition for converting speech to text in addition to Natural Language Understanding (NLU.)

Lex works like LUIS, in that it identifies intents (what the goal of the user is), interprets the user input phrases (called Utterances), determines the data needed to fulfill the intent (called Slots) and then runs the fulfillment methods to complete the intent.

One of the advantages of using Lex is it also provides easier integration to Amazon Alexa by adding new skills. Amazon also provides a service called Amazon Polly, which converts text to speech.

Apache OpenNLP

Apache offers an open source framework for NLP including language detection, sentence detection, name/entity recognition, and categorization.

Apache OpenNLP is typically used to normalize speech (for example changing dogs to dog) and is used in combination with other deep learning libraries for analysis.

Challenges with NLP

When building an NLP application, the initial step after data extraction (which in itself could be challenging depending on your system of record) is to create a corpus, which is the text record of information specific to your industry or company. In a med-tech company, this would be the categorization of language related to your specific medical expertise. In retail, it could be a list of skus and descriptions of products. Creating a corpus for a company is a lengthy process that can take a month or longer to develop. Additionally, when implementing them initially, a person performing the review may not identify all keywords accordingly so once the corpus is implemented a process to update the corpus and re-train the data needs to be put in place for subsequent updates.

This is one advantage that a framework such as IBM Watson or Microsoft LUIS has is that it can suggest new entries into the corpus based on the context.

A second challenge with NLP technologies is context-specific requests. Most solutions in the market look for keyword patterns to identify the response or recommended action. The challenge with this is that many of them don't take into account the previous dialogue when determining a response which can lead to a very frustrating experience from an end user perspective.

Examples

Natural language processing has been used in several different solutions and the most often referenced example is in spam filters. Google uses natural language understanding to power it's Google Translate service.

Lum.ai is a startup based out of the University of Arizona's which allows researchers to identify relationships for a keyword across multiple articles along with keyword context metrics. For example, a researcher using Lum with searching for one protein (HLA-G) can also see relationships with other proteins from other articles ('HLA-G inhibits NK Cells'). The benefit of this is that a researcher can instantly see all related published articles and can then make an informed decision on how to proceed or change a test based on already published research. The advantage to this is that a researcher can instantly see related research without reviewing hundreds of documents returned by a keyword search.

Some of the challenges the Lum team identified when creating their platform was the lack of information on cancer research corpuses. To solve this, they created a grammar pattern-based algorithm to create their corpus automatically based on grammar rules specific to medical research documentation.

Data Scientist Jordan Bramble created a sentiment analysis using Twitter data[3] to identify which states were the happiest. Through the Twitter API he pulled 23,000 random tweets, created a dictionary of US cities and towns, and then did a sentiment analysis on the data. Through that analysis he identified that Utah is the happiest state while Wyoming has the lowest score.

By using NLP as part of your strategic competence you can identify new insights regarding your marketing effectiveness, and customer service issues reported not only for your company but also for those of your competitors (which may lead to some interesting viral marketing opportunities if you can solve the problem for a person complaining about your competitor.)

Companies expanding NLP[3] capabilities in their organizations are focus are for customer service question answering, reputation monitoring, ad placement, competitive intelligence (hedge funds routinely use NLP in their models), and regulatory compliance.

Notes

[1] https://cloud.google.com/natural-language/

[2] https://medium.com/@JBramVB/mapping-happiness-with-twitter-natural-language-processing-ac231e70fe7

[3] https://www.techemergence.com/natural-language-processing-business-applications/

CHAPTER 9

I've Been Vetted Case Study

I've Been Vetted (IBV) is a company headquartered in Phoenix, Arizona and is the first post-employment risk mitigation platform. Jo Lynn Clemens, CEO has a background in risk mitigation for over 20 years. She states that in traditional risk management systems, employee risk monitoring stops once a background check is complete. The IBV system continually monitors employee risk factors by integrating with employer HR Management systems, recurring background checks, reviewing licensing systems, and monitoring social media platforms such as Twitter and Facebook for keywords and groups that indicate criminal or risky behavior.

In their analytics and data visualization platform, they identify and predict possible issues with individual employee risk factors that might damage a company's reputation. They also focus on risk factors group by geo-location information that might indicate issues with leadership in a specific region, district, or location.

As a company, one of the challenges in their service offering is the fine line between employee privacy and risk mitigation. Their platform follows the standards set by government agencies for risk profile flagging based on keyword analytics.

IBV CTO Ashesh Kapur chose Python/Spark/Hadoop as his technology platform of choice. He states "We chose these technologies because of the ease of use, the libraries available and the expertise is available in the market." He believes a Spark framework gives them faster real-time analytics than what Hadoop processing provides natively.

When implementing AI technologies, Ashesh stated that a large part of the project was invested in data cleansing, preparation, data quality analysis, and staging of the data. His advice to companies who are implementing AI technologies is "Ensure you are working to identify quality data sources, invest in data quality and to not build a humongous system out of the gate." He also feels that Hadoop offers a great database platform for scalable systems.

Jo Lynn states that her company offers the same risk management processes that insurance companies currently use for optimizing their insurance risk prediction algorithms and transfers this to private enterprises. This gives businesses the same capabilities to assess and monitor risk of their employees to deter reputational damage, criminal activity, and legal action.

CHAPTER 10

JP Morgan Case Study

In June of 2016 JP Morgan rolled out a new AI project that saved them 360,000 hours of lawyer's time annually. The project, called COIN for Contract Intelligence automates the process for commercial loan agreements.

The JP Morgan system uses a combination of AI and robots to automate loan servicing for over 12,000 contracts. The project also reduced mistakes from human error.

JP Morgan visited high tech companies such as Apple and Facebook in 2013 to gain more insight into machine learning and big data efforts. They created their own computing cloud called Gaia that enables JP Morgan to add new systems in their private cloud and has created hubs in their organization for machine learning and AI technologies[1].

They are actively working on deploying the technology in other ways and in January 2017 deployed an AI system called X Connect which enables the company to read employee emails and identify connections to potential customers within their employee network.

JP Morgan invests roughly 33% of their technology spend in new initiatives with a goal to get to 40% soon.

JP Morgan actively invests in automation and has created bots that manage IT requests such as resetting passwords. JP Morgan's COO Matt Zames states that these bots are expected to handle 1.7 million requests annually and perform the work of 140 people[2].

At JP Morgan's investor day, they highlighted their investment in technology capabilities and are leaders in the market relative to their peers in technology spend.

JP Morgan's CIO Dana Deasy states "Anything where you have back-office operations and humans kind of moving information from point A to point B that's not automated is ripe for that [automation]. People always talk about this stuff as displacement. I talk about it as freeing people to work on higher-value things, which is why it's such a terrific opportunity for the firm."

Notes

[1] http://www.independent.co.uk/news/business/news/jp-morgan-software-lawyers-coin-contract-intelligence-parsing-financial-deals-seconds-legal-working-a7603256.html

[2] https://www.bloomberg.com/news/articles/2017-02-28/jpmorgan-marshals-an-army-of-developers-to-automate-high-finance

Chapter 11

Eddie the Sales Robot

Eddie is my own robot (and an employee of my company) that handles my prospecting. (I thought it was just slightly genius to build a robot to sell robot services!) Eddie is built using UI Path and every day he does the following things for me:

1. He reviews LinkedIn navigator to see if there's anyone that I've added to our lead list that hasn't been contacted. If he finds a new lead, he contacts them with a special message.
2. If there's no new leads, he reviews LinkedIn navigator looking for C-level employees and VP employees.
3. He identifies 10 different leads and searches our CRM to see if we've contacted them previously.
4. He chooses 2 of those contacts based on the following factors: do they have any type of connection to someone in my company and has their competitor hired an RPA developer.
5. He has 2 different email campaigns that we are A/B testing and emails one of each.

6. He views the other 8 contact profiles.
7. He documents all of this in our CRM system.
8. Then he logs this into a custom database that we'll use later to integrate into machine learning algorithms.

The next thing Eddie does during the day is reviews his responses from previous companies. If someone replies with a standard 'I'd like to meet' type of response, he contacts Amy to set up an appointment. If he doesn't understand the response, he forwards it to another person on the team to take care of.

When designing Eddie, I needed to consider several different things:
1. What was the information that I wanted Eddie to search (basically repeating a human process).
2. What was the information that I wanted Eddie to track that I can use for machine learning later?
3. With LinkedIn, you get a limited set of inmails, so how could I maximize which person I connect to?
4. How could I test Eddie's effectiveness for his sales automation campaign?

By adding data to a custom database (instead of just storing it in a CRM system), I'm able to collect information very quickly that can be used in machine learning algorithms to determine if a lead is likely to respond.

Eddie saves me dozens of hours a week on my sales prospecting and only took me a few days to set up. He's the best employee I've ever had.

CHAPTER 12

Next Steps

I hope that this book has gotten you excited about the possibilities that AI offers. And if you aren't excited, then you should be fearful. If you aren't planning your AI projects now, you are very soon going to be at a huge disadvantage regarding competitiveness in your industry.

Robots give you highly accurate manpower at a low cost. AI gives you data-centric decision making capability at any level in the organization. Companies leveraging their data can make better decisions and companies leveraging their employees on higher-valued tasks can create real opportunities for innovation.

To be successful, it will require forward-thinking leaders to promote the benefits. It will require that employees change the way that they do their jobs. It's going to require HR teams to step up to the plate to do more with their employees – whether that's retraining or reorgs.

These massive shifts aren't coming, they are here. Companies taking advantage of the benefits are seeing the results.

Machine Learning and AI are not the exclusive domain of huge high-tech companies. These technologies are within reach to companies of any size. Find a data scientist, give them your data, and get ready to go! These technologies are complex and the talent is hard to find, but companies at any size can now participate.

Even my own robot assistant makes my small company more efficient and I'm constantly dreaming of the robots I can create that improves my operations. My robot army is just beginning. The next level: my robot army powered by AI makes my company a threat to large organizations.

As a business owner, my goal is to have a 50% digital workforce that augments my teams, sells my products, monitors my competitors, and promotes my articles.

The robots are here and they are making companies more efficient, more effective, and reducing costs. With every replacement hire, executives should be asking the question, can a robot do this job? If the answer is yes, what are you waiting for?

If you look at the history of tech change, when the internet came around, everyone needed a website. When apps became a thing, everyone needed an app. When marketing automation became a thing, everyone needed to automate their marketing.

RPA is a game-changing technology, and everyone should be leveraging it. More productivity at a fraction of the cost of an employee? Sound like a must-have for any organization to me.

If you have a database, you need AI. It's a major differentiator that can set you apart if you take the time to experiment, understand it, and leverage it.

ABOUT THE AUTHOR

Crystal Taggart is a technology consultant specializing in AI and RPA technologies. Her IT career spans 20 years with experience ranging from Startups to Fortune 500 companies. She holds a degree in Global Business from Arizona State University and an MBA from the University of Arizona.

She is the author of four books including *How to Hire an Offshore Developer and Launch Your Startup, Using Axure 7 RP Pro, Zendesk Quickstart Guide: The Step-by-Step Guide to create ITIL Processes*, and *Learning Self Service: Tools and Techniques for Online Learning Design*.

You can reach her at c.taggart@atlasinnovations.com.

www.ingramcontent.com/pod-product-compliance
Lightning Source LLC
Chambersburg PA
CBHW070309230526
45470CB00002B/799